CTA
His Message. Your Mission.

CRUCIFIED GLORIFIED

Rodney L. Rathmann

*While we were yet sinners,
Christ died for us.*
Romans 5:8 *KJV*

Devotional Prayer Journal

The vision of CTA is
to see Christians highly effective
in their ministry so that Christ's Kingdom
is strengthened and expanded.

CRUCIFIED
GLORIFIED

Rodney L. Rathmann

Copyright © 2019 CTA, Inc.
1625 Larkin Williams Rd.
Fenton, MO 63026
www.CTAinc.com

PRINTED IN THAILAND
ISBN: 978-1-947699-07-6

CRUCIFIED
GLORIFIED

With his Word, God
called creation into
existence. Then God
sent his only Son, the
Word made flesh, to set
into motion and fulfill his
plan for human salvation.
God's written Word tells
us about our Savior—
promised, incarnate,
and offered up
for us in a life
of obedience and
sacrifice. Through this
same Word, God's Spirit
brings us to faith and gives us
the strength to live each day as
people of God.

The devotional materials in
this book invite you to apply
God's Word as you reflect
upon what Jesus' sacrifice
and ultimate victory means
for you, here and now.
Organized chronologically,

the daily Bible readings draw attention to the things Jesus taught and experienced beginning with Palm Sunday and ending with Easter morning. To complete each day, you'll find a journaling opportunity to bring focus, organization, and clarity to your thoughts.

In addition to the 40 daily devotions, you'll find six Sunday interludes designed to lead you in worshipping and praising our glorious God and Savior. The final pages record some powerful words of Scripture, words that emphasize what Jesus' death and resurrection mean in the life of the believer.

May you grow closer to our Savior, crucified and glorified, as you spend the next six weeks with him in his Word!

Day 1: Ash Wednesday
From Sinner to Saint

Read Luke 9:18–24.

The Son of Man must be delivered into the hands of sinful men and be crucified and on the third day rise.

Luke 24:7

For Reflection: Today, many people around the world will gather for worship. Some will receive ashes, applied to their foreheads in the shape of a cross, as they hear the words, "For you are dust, and to dust you shall return" (Genesis 3:19). These words, spoken to Adam after he sinned in the Garden of Eden, remind us of our heritage of sin and death. But wait, there is Good News here! In Jesus' cross we find forgiveness and a new, glory-filled identity. Today, write about what the totality of the Passion story—Jesus' rejection, suffering, crucifixion, and resurrection—means for you.

Thank you, Jesus, for coming to earth to live, suffer, and die for me. Thank you for the grace and forgiveness you give. As I prepare for Easter, help me to . . .

Day 2: Thursday
Glory in Death

The Word became flesh and dwelt among us, and we have seen his glory, glory as of the only Son from the Father, full of grace and truth.

John 1:14

For Reflection: Basking in the glory that is his rightful due, the Son of God enters Jerusalem. With the fanfare reserved for a conquering hero-king, the crowds greet Jesus with palm branches and shouts of "Hosanna!" They honor him in recognition of his raising of Lazarus from the dead. Then, looking ahead to his own death and glorious resurrection, Jesus teaches about life, death, and discipleship. "Unless a grain of wheat falls into the earth and dies, it remains alone," Jesus says, "but if it dies, it bears much fruit" (John 12:24). Write about the meaning of these words in Jesus' life and in yours.

Savior, I give you all glory and honor.
You died to bring me new life. Let me die to myself so that
I may glorify you in all I do. May I live for you as I . . .

Day 3: Friday
In the Father's House

O LORD, I love the habitation of your house and the place where your glory dwells.

Psalm 26:8

For Reflection: Abraham and Sarah entertained God himself when he visited them, having taken on human form (Genesis 18:1–15). There is something wonderful and awesome about the hospitality God shows us when we come to his house, too. His glory dwells there, and it is there that we come into contact with his Word. There we receive the forgiveness, strength, and healing only his Son, the Word made flesh, can provide. In today's reading, Jesus expressed frustration with those who mocked and misused God's house. But how he must have delighted in the children's shouts of praise! Write about a worship experience in which you received a special blessing.

_____

_____

_____

_____

_____

_____

Hosanna to the Son of David! I join with children who long ago worshipped you and praised your holy name. I look forward to the day I will live in my Father's house forever. I think about . . .

Day 4: Saturday
Glory Two Ways

Read Luke 20:19–26.

But our citizenship is in heaven, and from it we await a Savior, the Lord Jesus Christ, who will transform our lowly body to be like his glorious body, by the power that enables him even to subject all things to himself.

Philippians 3:20–21

For Reflection: As the time drew near for Jesus to die for the sins of the world, his enemies sought to trap him with a question about taxes. Jesus' answer reminds us that as his forgiven children, we are called to live in two worlds. We owe our allegiance to God. Yet as followers of Jesus, we glorify our heavenly Father when we serve others as good neighbors and faithful citizens. Considering your own life, write about the opportunities and challenges you see when giving glory to God in both ways.

Dear Jesus, I know my citizenship is in heaven even now, but I also live each day in a fallen world. Give me grace as I navigate between the two worlds and help me give glory to you by . . .

First Sunday in Lent

Many Christians around the world participate in 40 days of personal reflection and repentance just before Easter. Sometimes called Lent, this time of preparation excludes the six Sundays that fall during this period. Thus, every Sunday—even the Sundays in Lent—call us to celebrate the resurrection of our Savior.

Today, reflect on God's glory and grace in your life by meditating on the words of the following hymn verse, one that has been sung by Christians down through the centuries on Palm Sunday:

All glory, laud, and honor to you, Redeemer, King.
To whom the lips of children made sweet hosannas ring.
As you received their praises, accept the prayers we bring.
O source of every blessing, our good and gracious King.

Theodulf, Bishop of Orléans (c. 820)
Translator: J. M. Neale (1854)

Day 5: Monday
Questions

But when the fullness of time had come, God sent forth his Son, born of woman, born under the law, to redeem those who were under the law, so that we might receive adoption as sons.

Galatians 4:4–5

For Reflection: Sources attribute the popular catchphrase "That's the $64,000 question" to a 1940s CBS radio show called *Take It or Leave It*. Contestants on this show answered increasingly difficult questions as the amount of prize money doubled with each new question. Just days before his death on the cross, Jesus asks his listeners two "64,000 dollar" questions: "What do you think about the Christ? Whose son is he?" (Matthew 22:42). Then, referring to Scriptures, Jesus identifies the Messiah as David's Son, being true man, and David's Lord, being true God. Yes, the Baby once born in a lowly manger is our King! What does it mean in your own life that Jesus is truly and fully both God and human? Write about that here.

_____

_____

_____

_____

_____

My Savior, how wonderful you are! You are almighty God, but you took on frail humanity. As a true human being, you died for my sins. As the sinless Son of God, you made me holy in the sight of my Father. I praise you, Savior, because . . .

Day 6: Tuesday
A Widow's Offering

Read Mark 12:41–44.

And he died for all, that those who live might no longer live for themselves but for him who for their sake died and was raised.

2 Corinthians 5:15

For Reflection: Artists have painted the widow we read about in Mark 12 gazing downward as one hand drops her humble offering into the collection box and the other holds the hand of a small child. Scripture makes no mention of a child, but it does tell us that the woman's sacrificial gift caught our Savior's attention in the final days before his own sacrifice on the cross. With a selflessness that foreshadows our Savior's own offering on Calvary, this widow's tithe was 100 percent; she gave everything she had. What does Jesus' offering mean to you? In what specific ways can you go all in for him in the things you do today? Write about that here.

I thank and praise you, Savior, for you are the ultimate Giver. You can do mighty things through my humble acts of giving. Help me to be more generous in . . .

Day 7: Wednesday
All That Remains

You, Lord, laid the foundation of the earth in the beginning, and the heavens are the work of your hands; they will perish, but you remain; they will all wear out like a garment. . . . But you are the same, and your years will have no end.

Hebrews 1:10–12

For Reflection: It's not a very reassuring statement: "Heaven and earth will pass away" (Luke 21:33). We can hardly bear to imagine everything being taken away. Our wealth, our family, our life—there would be nothing left—except the Word of God and your faith in Jesus. No matter what this earthly life brings, all of Jesus' promises are certain. The grace, mercy, and forgiveness he offers have no end! And, your Savior will return one day to take you to the mansion he has prepared (John 14:2). Not even death on a cross and three days in a tomb could stop him. Write about the ways you might intentionally live your life in light of Jesus' promise to come again.

_____

_____

_____

_____

_____

Lord, grant me the wisdom to see your promises as the eternal truth. As I look forward to the day when you take me to live with you forever, may I . . .

Day 8: Thursday
Watch!

Read Matthew 25:1–13.

The kingdom of God is at hand; repent and believe in the gospel.

Mark 1:15

For Reflection: "Give me oil in my lamp, keep me burning." So goes the traditional children's song based on Jesus' parable of the ten bridesmaids. Coincidently, the chorus of this song echoes the praises sung at Jesus' Palm Sunday parade, "Hosanna to the King of kings!" The oil in the lamp symbolizes faith in our crucified and glorified Savior. With faith burning in our hearts, we will be ready for Jesus, our Bridegroom, when he comes to take us into his heavenly home. Think about the people around you who do not yet possess "oil in their lamps." Reflect on your opportunities to bring them the Good News so that, by the Holy Spirit's power, they too may be ready to go with Jesus when he comes again.

My Savior, kindle the fire of faith and keep it burning in my heart. Keep me ever ready as I await your coming. Help me to make the most of faith-sharing opportunities, especially with . . .

Day 9: Friday
You're Invited!

Read Matthew 22:1–14.

For God so loved the world, that he gave his only Son, that whoever believes in him should not perish but have eternal life.

John 3:16

For Reflection: Many of Jesus' teachings during the week of his death underscore God's free gift of salvation. Those teachings also include words of warning and admonition. Today's parable is no exception. Through the gift of his Son, God offers everyone a banquet of good things, both now and in his coming Kingdom. His invitation remains open to all. Still many reject his generosity and refuse to put their trust in him. Ponder for a moment God's invitation to you. Write your response below in the form of an RSVP.

_____

_____

_____

_____

_____

_____

Heavenly Father, you want all to know you and to come to a knowledge of the truth. What a feast you have prepared for me! Today I thank you especially for . . .

Day 10: Saturday
Ever Ready

Be faithful unto death, and I will give you the crown of life.

Revelation 2:10

For Reflection: It is said that we show our true selves by the things we do when we think no one is watching. To Christians, this means we remain obedient and faithful to Jesus even as those around us live to satisfy their selfish, self-centered longings. Too often, though, we succumb to the same temptations as those around us. Even so, our Savior freely offers us the forgiveness he won for us on Calvary's cross. Just as surely as he defeated death that very first Resurrection Day, so too he will strengthen us to live for him as we await his coming again. Write your thoughts about faith, forgiveness, and the "crown of life" Jesus has waiting for you.

_____

_____

_____

_____

_____

_____

**My Savior, the burdens and joys of daily life fill my mind.
I care too much about fitting in with those around me.
Forgive me and remind me of the glorious inheritance
you have secured for me. Grow my faith as I . . .**

Jesus' teaching during the week of his crucifixion focuses on the awesome, happy day when he will come again in glory. Jesus has told us to prepare and watch for that day. The verses of the following hymn anticipate Jesus' second coming. What happy thoughts come to mind when you pray, "Come quickly, King of kings"?

The King shall come when morning dawns
  and light triumphant breaks,
When beauty gilds the eastern hills
  and life to joy awakes.

Oh, brighter than that glorious morn
  shall dawn upon our race.
The day when Christ in splendor comes
  and we shall see his face.

The King shall come when morning dawns
  and light and beauty brings.
Hail, Christ the Lord! Your people pray:
  Come quickly, King of kings!

John Brownlie (1859–1925)

Guilt and Innocence (Week 3)

Day 11: Monday
The Final Separation

Read Matthew 25:31–46.

And just as it is appointed for man to die once, and after that comes judgment, so Christ, having been offered once to bear the sins of many, will appear a second time, not to deal with sin but to save those who are eagerly waiting for him.

Hebrews 9:27–28

For Reflection: In today's Passion-week teaching, Jesus says that the loving acts of faith done to even the least among us are done to Jesus himself. It follows then that we also serve God by gratefully allowing others to perform loving acts for us. This double take on serving God can be a special comfort for those who, by reason of age or illness, are no longer able to care for others in Christian service as they once did. How can you "be Jesus" today in the things you do for others and in the things you allow others to do for you?

Jesus, I'm guilty of turning away "the least of these" (Matthew 25:45). But, you have taken my guilt upon yourself and given me your innocence. Help me see *you* when I look at myself and others so that I may . . .

17

Day 12: Tuesday
A Grateful Act of Worship

Bless the LORD, O my soul, and all that is within me, bless his holy name!

Psalm 103:1

For Reflection: With the exuberance of David as he danced before the Lord (2 Samuel 6:12–19), this woman of Bethany worshipped her Savior with abandon, boldly anointing Jesus with expensive perfume. Bible scholars think the woman may have been Mary, Martha's sister, who had already shown her devotion to Jesus once before (Luke 10:38–42). Jesus had recently raised Mary's brother, Lazarus, from the dead. Perhaps this was an act of humility from Mary, an outpouring of her thankfulness and praise. Either way, the disciples deemed the woman guilty of wasting a precious resource, but not Jesus. Jesus commended her. List a few specific reasons for praising and glorifying your God and Savior today.

_____

_____

_____

_____

_____

**Heavenly Father, you have given me all that I have
and made me all that I am. I anoint you with my praises
today. I come to you with humble thanksgiving for . . .**

Day 13: Wednesday
The Path of Salvation

Read Matthew 26:1–5, 14–16.

As for you, you meant evil against me, but God meant it for good.

Genesis 50:20

For Reflection: Incentivized by 30 pieces of silver, Judas Iscariot plots with Jesus' enemies to deliver the King of kings into their hands outside the public eye. This action echoes that of the patriarchs who, centuries before, sold their brother Joseph into slavery in Egypt (Genesis 37:28). If we are honest with ourselves, we are all guilty of putting our own interests above the needs of others, even those who are closest to us. But we have a great God! Just as he saved his Old Testament people through Joseph (Genesis 50:15–20), he ultimately turned Judas' betrayal into salvation for all believers through Jesus' suffering and death on the cross. When has God worked good through evil in your life? Write about that here.

Gracious God, you always bring about good for your people, even in the worst circumstances. In my life, you have taken the wickedness of my sins and given me, in its place, the purity of Christ's innocence. I praise you . . .

19

Day 14: Thursday
Together in Jesus

Read Luke 22:7–15.

And they devoted themselves to the apostles' teaching and the fellowship, to the breaking of bread and the prayers.

Acts 2:42

For Reflection: The night before he died, Jesus told his disciples, "I have earnestly desired to eat this Passover with you before I suffer" (Luke 22:15). Jesus sought to be near his friends because his time was near—he would soon take all of our guilt to the cross and die the death of a criminal. In a similar vein, believers throughout the years have regularly sought support and comfort from other Christians as they face death, illness, or other hardships. Think of a time when you earnestly desired the special assurance of God's care for you and you received that assurance by coming together with other believers. Write about it below.

Precious Savior, you have taken my sins away—erasing the charges against me and declaring me innocent. This comfort endures even in the midst of life's toughest situations, like . . .

Day 15: Friday
An Awesome Meal

Read 1 Corinthians 11:23–26.

For as often as you eat this bread and drink the cup, you proclaim the Lord's death until he comes.

1 Corinthians 11:26

For Reflection: A page in one family cookbook provides the recipe for potato soup together with the following annotation: "We regularly ate potato soup during the lean years of the Great Depression. In spite of having it so often, our whole family loved it and continued to serve it even after." Eating this meal, even many years after the Depression, brought a reassuring comfort. When believers share the Lord's Supper today, they remember a series of painful events. But still, "the whole family" loves it. Write about that here.

_____

_____

_____

_____

_____

_____

_____

Dear Jesus, the first Lord's Supper was just the beginning. When I remember how you suffered and died for me, I remember your all-forgiving grace and mercy. Your death made me spotless and righteous before God. Reassure me . . .

Day 16: Saturday
A Model for Servanthood

Read John 13:1–35.

The Son of Man came not to be served but to serve, and to give his life as a ransom for many.

Matthew 20:28

For Reflection: In today's reading, Jesus provides an object lesson on serving for his disciples, and for us. As his innocent hands washed the disciples' feet, Jesus stooped to become their servant. Just hours later, the disciples would witness Jesus' greatest act of servanthood—his hanging on a cruel wooden cross as he died in our place. The words he spoke later on that Passover night remind us of how we serve him. "By this all people will know that you are my disciples, if you have love for one another" (John 13:35). How can you show that you are a follower of Jesus in the things you do for others today?

Jesus, you are the ultimate Servant.
Your undying love for me, a guilty sinner, led you to
suffer on the cross. You redeemed me and now I serve
you by serving others. Help me to love others as I . . .

Third Sunday in Lent

The feast of the Passover commemorates the night when God saved his people in Egypt by "passing over" houses on which appeared the blood of a Lamb that had been sacrificed (Exodus 13:1–10). On the night of his betrayal when Jesus celebrated the Passover meal with his disciples, he identified himself as the new Passover Lamb. Praise God in the words of the following hymn of the ancient church, which celebrates Jesus as the one final Passover sacrifice.

At the Lamb's high feast we sing
    praise to our victorious King,
Who has washed us in the tide
    flowing from his pierced side.

Mighty Victim from the sky,
    hell's fierce pow'rs beneath you lie;
You have conquered in the fight.
    You have brought us life and light.

Translator: Robert Campbell (1849)

Punishment and Freedom (Week 4)

Day 17: Monday
God's Will Is Done

Read Matthew 26:36–46.

Your will be done, on earth as it is in heaven.

Matthew 6:10

For Reflection: The Bible reminds us that when considering our future intentions, we do well to add, "If the Lord wills" (James 4:15). Jesus agonized about God's will as he prayed in Gethsemane. As true God, Jesus knew what the coming hours held. Because Jesus shares our humanity, we can understand his feelings in anticipation of the rejection, humiliation, pain, and—finally—death he would endure to fulfill his Father's will. But above all, Jesus knew God's desire for "all people to be saved and to come to the knowledge of the truth" (1 Timothy 2:4). Consider God's will for a moment, and then write about how he is accomplishing it, right now, in your life.

Heavenly Father, you sent your Son to endure my punishment and earn my freedom. May I use that freedom to accomplish your will in my life. Guide me today as I . . .

Day 18: Tuesday
A Friend in Deed

Read Mark 14:32–42.

There is a friend who sticks closer than a brother.

Proverbs 18:24

For Reflection: Though we set out intending to live for Jesus, all too soon our mind entertains wrong thoughts, our tongue utters words that hurt, our feet bring us places we should not go, and our hands move in self-serving directions. It's as though the parts of our body are waging a war against the good we would like to do (Romans 7:21–25). In the disciples' case, they yielded to fatigue and fell asleep soon after Jesus, in agony and distress, asked them to watch and pray. In contrast, Jesus suffers the ultimate punishment upon the cross for them, showing himself to be the truest of friends. What thoughts come to mind when you think about his friendship?

_____

_____

_____

_____

_____

_____

**Dear Jesus, you are a perfect Friend to me. By your cross,
I am freed from Satan's grasp. Forgive me for the
many times I failed to be a faithful friend to you.
Help me to honor your faithful friendship by . . .**

25

Day 19: Wednesday
Betrayal

Read Matthew 26:47–50 and 27:3–10.

Finally, be strong in the Lord and in the strength of his might. Put on the whole armor of God, that you may be able to stand against the schemes of the devil.

Ephesians 6:10–11

For Reflection: We don't know exactly how the devil gained control in the life of Judas before he betrayed our Lord. Scripture hints at greed. Just days before, when Mary anointed Jesus with expensive perfume, Judas criticized her actions under the ruse that the money would've been better spent on the poor (John 12:3–8). Judas made this remark, not because he cared about the poor but because he was a thief. Just as with Judas, the devil works tirelessly to capture and control us. But, for followers of Jesus, Satan's schemes are powerless as we rely on our Savior for wisdom and support. Today, praise God for his saving, protecting power in your life.

I thank and praise you, Holy Spirit, for the salvation Jesus earned for me and for your strength in my life. Free from sin and Satan's power, I ask you to keep me strong to . . .

Day 20: Thursday
The Savior Denied

Read Luke 22:54–62.

For I am not ashamed of the gospel, for it is the power of God for salvation to everyone who believes, to the Jew first and also to the Greek.

Romans 1:16

For Reflection: Rooster figurines sit atop many church steeples in Europe. They serve as a reminder to stand strong against temptation and remain faithful to the Savior, whose faithfulness to God's people led him to the cross. In today's reading, a rooster's crow reminded Peter that his actions had strayed far from his best intentions (Luke 22:31–34). Just like Peter, we often fall short in our plans to live for our King. As you write today, confess these sins. Then, confident in Christ's forgiveness, finish the prayer that follows.

**Blessed Savior, you lived and died in my place.
Your hurt and humiliation broke the chains of sin,
freeing me from all that would lead me away from you.
Let me shout your praises as I . . .**

27

Day 21: Friday
Now Comes Mockery

Read Luke 22:63–65.

As obedient children, do not be conformed to the passions of your former ignorance, but as he who called you is holy, you also be holy in all your conduct, since it is written, "You shall be holy, for I am holy."

1 Peter 1:14–16

For Reflection: A popular British bakery chain once released an edgy Advent calendar showing three Wise Men gathered around a manger that contained a deli sandwich instead of the Baby Jesus. This is just one example of people in our culture who make light of God and his gifts. True, God is gracious, loving, and merciful. But God is also holy. He commands fear and respect. He punishes sin. As we read today, Jesus' enemies tormented, mocked, and made fun of him after his arrest. In the end, though, God will punish all who refuse the salvation for which his Son paid so dearly. As you write now, share your thoughts on God's holiness in light of both his justice and his grace.

_____

_____

_____

_____

_____

Heavenly Father, you are loving and merciful, but you hate sin. In Jesus' name, forgive me for the times I have misused your holy name and have not shown proper respect for you. Help me to choose a life of faithfulness to you by . . .

Day 22: Saturday
Keeping Perspective

Let us run with endurance the race that is set before us, looking to Jesus, the founder and perfecter of our faith, who for the joy that was set before him endured the cross, despising the shame, and is seated at the right hand of the throne of God.

Hebrews 12:1–2

For Reflection: Following his arrest, our Savior was tried before Annas and Caiaphas, men holding earthly jurisdiction over God's people. In a sense, Jesus is still on trial every day in our world. People ask, "Is there really a God? If there is a God, why doesn't he show himself more clearly? Where was he during the difficult times of my life?" Even the strongest believers sometimes ask questions like these. One thing is certain—God is real and he remains in control, even when we are tempted to doubt his power and presence. What does it mean to you that Jesus is seated at the right hand of God?

Jesus, my Savior, you are true man and true God. Remind me of that as doubts creep into my mind. With you by my side, I'm free to run the race that is set before me as I . . .

Fourth Sunday in Lent

Though blind, Fanny Crosby glorified God by writing more than 8,000 hymns and spiritual songs in her lifetime. God's blessings often find greatest appreciation in the midst of human struggles and challenges. Think about God's care during the trying times in your own life. Give God glory as you reflect on the following verse from one of Crosby's beloved hymns:

To God be the glory, great things he hath done,
So loved he the world that he gave us his Son,
Who yielded his life an atonement for sin,
And opened the life gate that all may go in.

Refrain:
Praise the Lord, praise the Lord, let the earth hear his voice!
Praise the Lord, praise the Lord, let the people rejoice!
Oh, come to the Father, through Jesus the Son,
And give him the glory, great things he hath done.

Day 23: Monday
The Truth of the Charges

Read Luke 23:1–5.

He came to his own, and his own people did not receive him. But to all who did receive him, who believed in his name, he gave the right to become children of God.

John 1:11–12

For Reflection: Most likely, the accusations levied against Jesus made little sense to Pilate, the Roman governor. To him, it seemed as though the leaders of the people had an agenda of their own. Had Jesus misled the nation by claiming to be the people's king? Pilate didn't see it: "I find no guilt in this man" (Luke 23:4). But the crowd wouldn't stop: "He stirs up the people, teaching throughout all Judea, from Galilee even to this place" (Luke 23:5). It's true—when Jesus enters our human existence, he does stir things up. Hearts change, lives change. The forgiveness, salvation, and new beginning he offers certainly stir people. Think about it—how has Jesus' victory over sin affected your life?

Jesus, when you entered the world, it changed.
When you entered my life, I changed. Lead me to
remember the victory you earned for me through your
pain and suffering. Stir up my heart, Lord, as I . . .

31

Day 24: Tuesday
In Search of a Miracle

Read Luke 23:6–16.

Jews demand signs and Greeks seek wisdom, but we preach Christ crucified, a stumbling block to Jews and folly to Gentiles.
1 Corinthians 1:22–23

For Reflection: Knowing Jesus was innocent, Pilate attempted to remove himself from the messy situation by sending Jesus to Herod, the Jewish ruler over Galilee. Herod had heard that Jesus could do miracles and, of course, he wanted to see one. Jesus certainly had the power to perform feats overriding the forces of nature. Yet, he refused. Jesus' divine miracles weren't some kind of sideshow. Instead, they were purposeful acts meant to demonstrate his authority to forgive and save. Soon enough, Herod would see the miracle—the miraculous suffering, death, and victory of Jesus on the cross. Write about how Jesus' suffering and death is a miracle in its own right.

Victorious Savior, you took my sins to the cross and accomplished the impossible—my salvation. As a forgiven child of God, I come before your throne of grace today asking you to once again do the impossible in my life by . . .

Day 25: Wednesday
A Pardon Received

Read Matthew 27:15–23.

God shows his love for us in that while we were still sinners, Christ died for us.

Romans 5:8

For Reflection: You probably imagine Barabbas as the paragon of evil, the hardened criminal, appearing grizzled, sly, and shifty. Scriptures, after all, describe him as a murderer and insurrectionist, a notorious prisoner. Yes, Pilate thought him a shoo-in solution for the "Jesus problem." In the eyes of God, Barabbas was much like us—totally at fault, guilty, and unworthy of rescue. Even so, Jesus took Barabbas's place, and your place, on the cross. He took all of the pain and suffering that you deserved. Consider what it means to you that Jesus took on the pain and death that should have been yours.

Jesus, you pardoned me from the guilt of my sins. Unworthy though I am, your victory on the cross is my victory! When I think about all you have done for me, I . . .

Day 26: Thursday
Behold the Man

Read Matthew 27:24–31.

Surely he has borne our griefs and carried our sorrows; yet we esteemed him stricken, smitten by God, and afflicted. But he was pierced for our transgressions; he was crushed for our iniquities; upon him was the chastisement that brought us peace, and with his wounds we are healed.

Isaiah 53:4–5

For Reflection: Some define *integrity* as doing the right thing even when it's difficult. In the readings from yesterday and today, we see Pilate's lack of integrity on full display. He refused to take responsibility for Jesus' fate, first by releasing Barabbas and then by shifting responsibility to the riled-up crowd. Finally and literally, Pilate washed his hands of the whole ugly affair and sentenced an innocent man to die. Jesus, on the other hand, continuously modeled integrity. He could have stopped his journey to the cross at any moment. But in obedience to the Father, he suffered in our place. Reflect upon integrity in light of Jesus' wounds and your healing.

Jesus, you suffered in order to redeem and save me. As I live through your victory, guide me to do the right thing even when it isn't easy. Enable me to serve you as I . . .

Pain and Victory (Week 5)

Day 27: Friday
Unexpected Cross Carrying

Read Mark 15:20–21.

If anyone would come after me, let him deny himself and take up his cross and follow me.

Mark 8:34

For Reflection: Today, we read that the man who carried Jesus' cross was named Simon, but we don't know much beyond that. Simon hadn't planned to meet Jesus. He was simply in the wrong place at the wrong time, and Rome's soldiers commandeered his service. That's how it often is when we encounter Jesus; he comes into our lives and we are never the same again. We see joy, pain, challenges, and victories in a totally new light. Oh, yes. We also know that Simon was the father of Alexander and Rufus. Perhaps Simon told them about the Savior he met unexpectedly that day. Perhaps they, together with their father, came to faith in him. In what unexpected ways has Jesus changed your life?

Thank you, heavenly Father, for sending Jesus to be my Savior. Keep me mindful of those who do not know Jesus yet. Help me show them the awesome ways Jesus' victory has changed my life . . .

35

Day 28: Saturday
What Is Truth?

Read John 19:18–22.

So Jesus said to the Jews who had believed him, "If you abide in my word, you are truly my disciples, and you will know the truth, and the truth will set you free."

John 8:31–32

For Reflection: Pilate's inscription, "Jesus of Nazareth, the King of the Jews," posted on the cross, gave offense to Jesus' enemies. Showing fortitude at last, Pilate refused to change it. Perhaps Pilate's determination on this issue somehow connects to an earlier conversation he had with Jesus about his Kingdom (John 18:33–38). Jesus told Pilate, "I have come into the world—to bear witness to the truth. Everyone who is of the truth listens to my voice" (verse 37). Pilate ended the interchange with the question, "What is truth?" (verse 38). Jesus' sacrifice and victory secured a place for you in the Kingdom of heaven. As a redeemed child of God, how would you answer Pilate's question?

_____

_____

_____

_____

_____

Jesus, I praise you for the victory you earned for me on the cross! Thank you for bringing me into your Kingdom. Through faith, I know the truth that sets me free. I celebrate this truth by . . .

Fifth Sunday in Lent

Grace is defined as "God's undeserved favor." A favorite Lenten hymn in some traditions, "Come to Calvary's Holy Mountain," pictures God's grace as a fountain flowing from the hill on which Jesus died. As you reflect on a verse from this hymn, praise God for the unending grace he offers.

Come to Calvary's Holy Mountain, sinners ruined by the fall;
Here a pure and healing fountain flows for you, for me, for all,
In a full, perpetual tide, opened when our Savior died.

They that drink shall live forever; 'tis a soul–renewing flood.
God is faithful; God will never break his covenant of blood.
Signed when our redeemer died, sealed when he was glorified.

James Montgomery (1854)

Lamb and King (Week 6)

Day 29: Monday
Self-Sacrificing Forgiveness

Read Luke 23:32–34.

Bearing with one another and, if one has a complaint against another, forgiving each other; as the Lord has forgiven you, so you also must forgive.

Colossians 3:13

For Reflection: The ability to give and receive forgiveness ultimately originates in the God who made us, saved us, and redirects us. In today's Bible reading, Jesus shows us the extent of his love and forgiveness. He served as a sacrificial lamb, enduring a death he didn't deserve. But, he wasn't resentful. He wasn't angry. Upon the cross, our King overflowed with love. While enduring the severest torment at the hand of his enemies, Jesus pleaded with his Father for their benefit, asking that they might be forgiven. Write about the forgiveness you have received from God and from others. Is there somebody who needs the gift of forgiveness from you today?

Jesus, Lamb of God, in love you took my place on the cross. You are my eternal King, freely offering forgiveness to cover all of my sins. Help me in turn to forgive . . .

Day 30: Tuesday
Prophecy Fulfilled

Read John 19:23–24.

You search the Scriptures because you think that in them you have eternal life; and it is they that bear witness about me.

John 5:39

For Reflection: Perhaps hardened by years of such events, the soldiers responsible for carrying out Jesus' crucifixion gambled for his clothing while the King of the Jews hung in agony. But it was more than a cruel game or diversion from military responsibilities. Hundreds of years before, David foretold this event in the words of Psalm 22:18, "They divide my garments among them, and for my clothing they cast lots." Every word of prophecy about the coming Savior was fulfilled in our King Jesus. Like our Savior himself, God's Word is totally reliable and trustworthy. On the lines below, write a passage of Scripture that is especially encouraging to you today. Then commit those words to memory.

Precious Lamb of God, you are God's promised Savior and you are my King. Every promise you have made to me is completely dependable. Today, help me remember your promise to . . .

39

Day 31: Wednesday
Mocking Words

Read Matthew 27:35–44.

He himself bore our sins in his body on the tree, that we might die to sin and live to righteousness. By his wounds you have been healed.

1 Peter 2:24

For Reflection: The well-known rhyme assures us that, unlike sticks and stones, words can never hurt us. But words do hurt. Some words do immeasurable damage. Hurtful bullying is not a new phenomenon. Seemingly everyone joined in as the dying Lamb of God was ridiculed, insulted, and mocked. The King of kings was taunted relentlessly—if he was truly God, he would stop everything and come down from the cross. More haunting still comes the phrase uttered mockingly, "He saved others, he cannot save himself" (Matthew 27:42). Why were people so cruel to the Sacrifice who had come in their place? Respond to all this here:

Heavenly Father, you gave your only Son as a sacrificial Lamb to suffer the cruelest of deaths for me. Because of him, you graciously forgive my cruel thoughts, words, and actions. Guide me to forgive others today, as I . . .

Day 32: Thursday
The Story of Three Crosses

The saying is trustworthy and deserving of full acceptance, that Christ Jesus came into the world to save sinners, of whom I am the foremost.

1 Timothy 1:15

For Reflection: The three crosses of Calvary tell the entire story of humanity. On the central cross, the innocent Lamb of God hangs. The punishment for our sins is heaped upon him. The other two crosses bear justly convicted criminals. While one criminal taunts and jeers his dying King, the other humbly begs, "Jesus, remember me when you come into your kingdom" (Luke 23:42). To this man Jesus speaks the words all the faithful yearn to hear on the day of their death, "Truly I say to you, today you will be with me in paradise" (Luke 23:43). What significances does the promise of this paradise have in your personal life?

_____

_____

_____

_____

_____

Dear Jesus, you are both Lamb and King. While some continue to mock you, I worship you and give you praise for the gift of salvation. Even today, I am living the eternal life you have given me by faith as I . . .

Day 33: Friday
Last Words

Read John 19:26–27.

Love bears all things, believes all things, hopes all things, endures all things.

1 Corinthians 13:7

For Reflection: Even while dying on the cross, Jesus showed care and concern for those closest to him, his mother and his friend John. His final words to them invited them to look upon each other as mother and son, and so they did. Jesus shows himself a faithful human son and friend, but Jesus is also God. No love compares to God's love. It melts the hardest of hearts, forgives the most grievous of offenses, and rebuilds the most devastated of lives. Going forward, how can God's love flow through you into the lives of the people God has placed in your life?

_____

_____

_____

_____

_____

Lamb of God, in your Word you show us how to love one another. Send your Holy Spirit to teach and empower me to honor you, the King of my life, in the love I show to others and . . .

Day 34: Saturday
Light in Darkness

Read Mark 15:33.

The people who walked in darkness have seen a great light; those who dwelt in a land of deep darkness, on them has light shone.

Isaiah 9:2

For Reflection: You don't have to be a follower of King Jesus to recognize good and evil as the two prevailing forces at work in the world. If light is associated with good and darkness with evil, it must have seemed that evil had the upper hand that dismal day in Palestine long ago. Yet down through the ages, that day has been referred to as Good Friday. Certainly, it was a good day for us. God's Son died on the cross, a sacrificial Lamb given to atone for all human sin. It's a wonder we don't call it "Great Friday." Write about how the light of Jesus overcomes the darkness in your world.

_____

_____

_____

_____

_____

_____

_____

Heavenly Father, in your Son, you sent a light that would burst through my sin-darkened existence. May that light shine brightly in my life as I . . .

43

Sixth Sunday in Lent (Palm Sunday)

Today begins the Christian observance of Holy Week. It starts out with Jesus' heroic ride into Jerusalem on Palm Sunday and ends with the celebration of Easter next Sunday. As we recall the events of this week, we reflect more deeply on Jesus' brutal and humiliating suffering and death to earn forgiveness and salvation for us. As we do so, we bear in mind both Jesus' passion and his triumph. Three stanzas of a well-known Palm Sunday hymn introduce the week's key themes.

Ride on, ride on in majesty! Hark! All the tribes hosanna cry.
O Savior meek, pursue thy road with palms and scattered
    garments strowed.

Ride on, ride on in majesty! In lowly pomp ride on to die.
O Christ, thy triumphs now begin o'er captive death and
    conquered sins.

Ride on, ride on in majesty! In lowly pomp ride on to die.
Bow thy meek head to mortal pain, then take, O God,
    thy pow'r and reign.

Henry Hart Milman (1827)

Joy and Sadness (Holy Week)

Day 35: Monday
The Cries of Jesus

Read Matthew 27:45–47.

For our sake he made him to be sin who knew no sin, so that in him we might become the righteousness of God.

2 Corinthians 5:21

For Reflection: How could God forsake his only Son during that Son's hour of greatest need? God rejected Jesus because, as Jesus hung on the cross, he became sin. Because of Jesus' sacrifice, we can rest assured that God will never reject us. Instead, he will go with us through all the struggles and changes we face. Deuteronomy 31:8 reminds us, "It is the LORD who goes before you. He will be with you; he will not leave you or forsake you." What struggles make you want to cry out to God today?

_____

_____

_____

_____

_____

_____

Dear God, Jesus took the curse that was rightly mine so that I could live in the joy of forgiveness. His death on Calvary's cross made me your friend! Strengthen me through my times of sadness that I might . . .

45

Day 36: Tuesday
Suffering

But rejoice insofar as you share Christ's sufferings, that you may also rejoice and be glad when his glory is revealed.

1 Peter 4:13

For Reflection: Jesus suffered in every way humanly possible before he died. His agonies were spiritual, emotional, and physical. Holding on to life, he gasped for breath to sustain his dehydrating body. Finally, after expressing the most basic of life-sustaining needs, Jesus is given wine vinegar to drink. But Jesus' thirst and its satisfaction was far from ordinary; it had been foretold by the psalmist long before (Psalm 69:21). Jesus' suffering was horrible. Still, its consequences are wonderful and far reaching! In the sadness, we can find joy. In what ways has Jesus brought joy from sadness in your life? Ponder these situations. Then write about them below.

Dear Savior, ever since sin came into the world, suffering has been part of the human experience. When you took on human form, you also took on suffering. As I endure sufferings in my life, may I find joy knowing . . .

Day 37: Wednesday
In the Hands of God

Read Luke 23:44–46 and John 19:30.

You take me out of the net they have hidden for me, for you are my refuge. Into your hand I commit my spirit; you have redeemed me, O LORD, faithful God.

Psalm 31:4–5

For Reflection: In today's Scripture passages, we hear Jesus' final words, echoing those of Psalm 31 (see above). After the temple curtain is torn, Jesus loudly prays his dying prayer, "Father, into your hands I commit my spirit" (Luke 23:46). The devil worked his hardest to thwart God's plans to save humanity, but Jesus prevailed. John's Gospel records the Savior's declaration of victory: "It is finished" (John 19:30). Then, Jesus took his final breath. He died, and our sins died with him. Capture the significance of this event in your own words here.

Father, you sent Jesus to buy me back from
Satan and from all that would condemn me.
It is finished—my sins are gone! What joy!
Lead me to rely on you and your faithfulness as I . . .

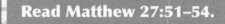
Day 38: Holy Thursday
The Centurion's Confession

Read Matthew 27:51–54.

The reason the Son of God appeared was to destroy the works of the devil.

1 John 3:8

For Reflection: Witnesses of the crucifixion saw some amazing things—the tearing of the temple curtain, an earthquake, and the resurrection of multiple, faithful believers. As he died, Jesus showed his ultimate power over death. Yes, there was sadness, but can you hear the awe as the centurion and others with him exclaim, "Truly this was the Son of God!" (Matthew 27:54)? Christians from some faith traditions refer to today as Maundy Thursday. *Maundy*, from the Latin word for "commandment," calls to mind Jesus' words to love one another (John 13:34). There is no better way to love others than to tell them about God's Son and the amazing things he has done. Whom will you tell?

Almighty and triune God, you made the world and you rule over all things. By your Spirit's power, help me fulfill your command to love others. Help me to be bold in proclaiming the Good News to . . .

Day 39: Good Friday
The Unblemished Sacrifice

Read John 19:31–37.

You were ransomed from the futile ways inherited from your forefathers, not with perishable things such as silver or gold, but with the precious blood of Christ, like that of a lamb without blemish or spot.

1 Peter 1:18–19

For Reflection: The word *excruciating* finds its origin in crucifixion, a most torturous form of execution. Usually its victims die from asphyxiation when they are no longer able to lift their sagging bodies to allow air to enter their lungs. The soldiers broke the legs of the two criminals, hastening their deaths. But when they came to Jesus, they saw he was already dead. They didn't break his legs, leaving him intact as the perfect, unblemished Sacrifice. They did, however, thrust a spear into his side, probably just below the ribs. This action likely punctured the area around the heart in which blood and water had collected. Jesus was truly dead. As you write, consider this cruel—yet perfect—death.

I love you, Jesus. Through the sadness of your excruciating death, you have brought me the joy of new life. Your love is perfect. Today may I show others that love by . . .

Day 40: Holy Saturday
A Hopeful Death

Read Matthew 27:57–66.

And you, who once were alienated and hostile in mind, doing evil deeds, he has now reconciled in his body of flesh by his death, in order to present you holy and blameless and above reproach before him.

Colossians 1:21–22

For Reflection: Refusing to believe Jesus had risen from the dead, some of the Lord's enemies would later refuse to acknowledge he had really died. They claimed he was asleep or had fainted, and then awakened. Jesus' death, however, is undeniable. The Roman soldiers assured and verified it; Jesus' followers affirmed it; Jesus' enemies took steps to prevent not an awakening but the theft of his dead body. For us, in the presence of a loved one who has died, the sad reality of death is all too obvious. Yet, for Jesus, death marked peace, release, and victory. Because we trust in Jesus, our death, as well as the death of believers around us, brings us the same hopeful joy. Reflect on these thoughts below.

_____

_____

_____

_____

My Savior, you died for me—a real, human death. Even though death brings sadness and sorrow, I can look through my tears and see the joy that lies ahead. Help me not to fear death, but to live confident that . . .

Joy and Sadness (Holy Week)

Resurrection Sunday
Alleluia! Christ Is Risen!

Read Matthew 28:1–8.

[Jesus said,] "I am the resurrection and the life. Whoever believes in me, though he die, yet shall he live, and everyone who lives and believes in me shall never die."

John 11:25–26

For Reflection: Jesus lives! Alleluia! Jesus' resurrection verifies that God has accepted Jesus' death on the cross as the full payment for all our sins. Jesus' resurrection turns all our sadness to joy. Jesus' resurrection makes us friends of God. Jesus' resurrection is the foundation for the Christian's faith, life, and hope! Write about what Jesus' resurrection victory means for your new life in him.

My Savior, the victory of Resurrection Sunday belongs to you! And by faith in you, it belongs to me! May I live the new life you give me with a Spirit-driven desire to . . .

51

Once Crucified, Now Glorified!

An empty cross, an empty tomb, a living Savior ...

In this is love, not that we have loved God but that he loved us and sent his Son to be the propitiation for our sins.

1 John 4:10

And if Christ has not been raised, then our preaching is in vain and your faith is in vain.

1 Corinthians 15:14

In fact Christ has been raised from the dead, the firstfruits of those who have fallen asleep.

1 Corinthians 15:20

For I know that my Redeemer lives, and at the last he will stand upon the earth.

Job 19:25

Being found in human form, [Jesus] humbled himself by becoming obedient to the point of death, even death on a cross.

Philippians 2:8

So is it with the resurrection of the dead. What is sown is perishable; what is raised is imperishable. It is sown in dishonor; it is raised in glory. It is sown in weakness; it is raised in power.

1 Corinthians 15:42–43

Jesus our Lord . . . was delivered up for our trespasses and raised for our justification.

Romans 4:24–25

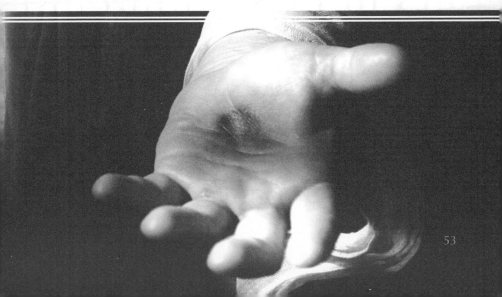

If we confess our sins, he is faithful and just to forgive us our sins and to cleanse us from all unrighteousness.

1 John 1:9

If you confess with your mouth that Jesus is Lord and believe in your heart that God raised him from the dead, you will be saved.

Romans 10:9

[He] was declared to be the Son of God in power according to the Spirit of holiness by his resurrection from the dead, Jesus Christ our Lord.

Romans 1:4

As it is written, "What no eye has seen, nor ear heard, nor the heart of man imagined, what God has prepared for those who love him."

1 Corinthians 2:9

Go therefore and make disciples of all nations, baptizing them in the name of the Father and of the Son and of the Holy Spirit, teaching them to observe all that I have commanded you. And behold, I am with you always, to the end of the age.

Matthew 28:19–20

*Blessed be the
God and Father of
our Lord Jesus Christ!
According to his great
mercy, he has caused
us to be born again to a
living hope through the
resurrection of Jesus Christ
from the dead, to an
inheritance that
is imperishable,
undefiled, and
unfading, kept in
heaven for you.*

1 Peter 1:3–4

To see all of CTA's devotion books and journals, visit us at www.CTAinc.com. You may order online or by calling 1-800-999-1874.

If this book has made a difference in your life or if you have simply enjoyed it, we would like to hear from you. Your words will encourage us!

Email: editor@CTAinc.com; include the subject line: CRG19PJ

Write: Editorial Manager, Department CRG19PJ
CTA, Inc.
PO Box 1205
Fenton, MO 63026-1205

Comment online: www.CTAinc.com
(search CRG19PJ)